TVSDK

The TV Self-Defense Kit

TVSDK:

TVSDK

SONY

The TV
Self-Defense
Kit

by Mike Haller

Houghton Mifflin Company Boston   1982

To Alice, for saying yes.
To Max, for being there.
To my parents, for enduring.

Library of Congress Cataloging in Publication Data

Haller, Mike.
  The TV self-defense kit.
  1. Television viewers — Anecdotes, facetiae, satire, etc. I. Title.
PN6231.T53H34   1982   791.45′0207   82-9225
ISBN 0-395-32931-0 (pbk.)   AACR2

Printed in the United States of America   P 10 9 8 7 6 5 4 3 2 1

TUBEQUOTES

The quotations printed within the tube-shaped boxes sprinkled throughout the book are called Tubequotes. Unlike the Portaquotes at the end of the book, these cannot be removed without damaging the continuity of the text or violating the United States Copyright Law.

I hope these quotations will inspire you to do further research into TV. If, in that process, you uncover any juicy tidbits, I'd love to see them. Send them to the address printed on page 80.

The quotation on page 8 is from "*TV Guide*'s First Annual J. Fred Muggs Awards," *TV Guide*, January 9, 1982.

On page 36, Dr. George Gerbner is quoted from "TV or Not TV," *Bill Moyers' Journal*, April 23, 1979 (show no. 412; library no. M-12). Les Brown's book *Television: The Business Behind the Box* was published by Harcourt, Brace, Jovanovich in 1971. Marshall McLuhan is quoted from his book *Understanding Media: The Extensions of Man* (New York: New American Library, 1964).

The quotation on page 38 is from *Brecht: The Man and His Work,* Doubleday, 1960.

The quotation on page 61 is from "TV or Not TV" (see above).

Book design: Mike Haller and Bob Overholtzer

Acknowledgments

Many people helped in the preparation of this book. Strangely, not a single one wanted his or her name associated with it. Despite this charming display of modesty, I feel compelled to mention some of them. For the moment, it's the most I can do to thank them.

Tom Hart, my editor, risked his career and his sanity with credible aplomb. The few times he was unavailable (out of town training for the snowshoe marathon) I turned to others for editorial consultation. Warner Marshall, Milena Jelinek, and Bill Lazarus were especially generous and helpful.

Many offered general encouragement at various crucial states: Herb and Beverly Chase, Kathy, Matthew, and Michael Fiveash (the curator of the Latin Hotline), Hillel Gedrich, Albert Gordon, Kim and Bill Haller, Judy Hardy, William Jelinek, Judy Mason, Garrett McCarey, Paul Milmed, June Mellies Reno, Penny and Jhan Robbins, Lee Savage, Beatrice Slotnick, Harvey and Joan Smith, and Polly Vorhaus. Rose Goldsen, a pioneer in the fight against TV addiction, opened her files to me.

Those who permitted me to photograph their TV-addicted lifestyles were Norman Garfield, Hal Moore, Bob Waldman, Jennifer Dolan, Joshua and Kate Dolan Waldman, Donna Santoro, Robin Slavin, Teena Grant, Roberta Klein, Jim Yantsos, Esther Bloom, Jim Louis, Chuck Stead, Joanna and Jim Weiss, Mark Rinis, John Telfer, Kate Telfer, Armen Merjanian, Christine Buonommo, Dan Sladkus, Anna and Veronica Gedrich, Timothy and Paul Sohn, Marisa and Jason Buzzeo, Sean McCarthy, Damien McGough, Micke, Hanna, David, and Pim Braunstein, Lauren Clark, Jennifer Georgi, Randy Carnefix, Susan Spaulding, Suzi Gursoy, and Prize Funk.

Mike Hardy was my photographic mentor and much more. Emilie Spaulding, my production manager, and Dan Sladkus, my photo assistant, were expert in the face of impossible odds. I'd also like to thank Vinnie and Estelle at Color Group (Hawthorne, N.Y.). Chip Lord, Dianne Hall, and M. D. McGowan provided stock photos. Thanks also go to the Nyack Bookstore, the Scuba Training & Equipment Center (West Nyack, N.Y.), Jersey Camera, Tarry Travel, and Miles Unlimited (Tarrytown, N.Y.), Stanton TV (Elmsford, N.Y.), St. John's Episcopal Church (New City, N.Y.), Bob's TV Service (Pleasantville, N.Y.), and Paula Tobin and the whole crew at Rockland Instant Copy. Lee Savage and Nancy Goldstein did the illustrations with an admirable sense of forbearance.

Extra special thanks are due to Rose Redding, Esther Bloom, Barbara Coleman, Randy Carnefix, and the dedicated members of the Elmwood Community Playhouse (Nyack, N.Y.). I deeply appreciate their tireless assistance.

TVSDK: The TV Self-Defense Kit
It's as Easy as ABC!

A. THE PROBLEM

HOW TO RECOGNIZE TV ADDICTION

"After watching three days of nothing but religious TV programming, a Phoenix handyman went berserk and shot his dog and his neighbor to death."

— *TV Guide*

A.1
Why You Need This Book

What did you do yesterday? You had twenty-four hours of time. So how did you spend it?

If you're an average person, you spent about eight hours **sleeping.** You spent another eight hours **working** (at a job, at home, or in school). I hope you spent at least two hours **eating** and **bathing.** And **traveling** probably took up another hour.

The four essentials of your life — **sleep, work, body maintenance,** and **travel** — ate up nineteen hours of your day. You had five hours of **leisure** time remaining before starting the whole cycle over. So what did you do? Let's look at the choices.

You could **read.** This includes anything from the *National Enquirer* to *War and Peace*. America has such a high literacy rate. It seems a shame to waste it.

You could **talk.** To your family, to your friends, or even to perfect strangers if that's what turns you on. The art of conversation is a great way to get things off your chest. The Greeks called it dialogue. Whatever you call it, it can be a genuinely uplifting experience.

You could **listen.** A major American corporation recently spent millions of dollars to convince us that it listens. For you, it can be much cheaper. Just stop talking for a few minutes.

You could **go out.** I know it's a hassle to find a parking space, but just think how much fun you'll have once you get where you're going. Besides, a change of scene is a sure-fire way to forget your troubles.

You could **do something.** I mean sports, hobbies, or whatever you want. This can be quite relaxing, and it solves the problem of what to do with your hands.

POWER
PULL ON
VOLUME

PICTURE

You could **read**   **talk**   **listen**   **go out**

LEISURE-TIME OPTIONS

You could **do nothing.** You might feel guilty at first, but remember, many famous people were expert at doing nothing. Walt Whitman said, "I loaf and invite my soul." This means that if you sit around and let your mind wander, you can have a real good time.

OK. I'll bet you can't wait to get going. But there is one more option I haven't mentioned.

You could **watch television.** This sounds a lot like doing nothing. But there are crucial differences. When you do nothing, your mind travels along a path of associations that actually help you work out your daily problems. (It's like jogging for the brain.) Freud called this free association.

When you watch television, you follow a path blazed by a small group of overpaid writers. Their job is to whip your mind into a frenzy of dramatic expectation every fifteen minutes or so and then cut to a commercial.

At this point another group of even higher-paid writers is brought in. They pester you with a sales pitch so attractively packaged that it's over before you have time to get another beer. Then they fling you back into the drama (or comedy, variety, or news) so the whole process can continue.

This is not free association. This is very expensive association.

do something   do nothing   or

watch TV

So how did you spend those five precious **leisure** hours? You didn't waste much of that time in front of the tube, did you?

Well, somebody did. Because last year in America, **every single man, woman, and child spent well over four hours a day watching TV.** This means YOU, Mr. or Ms. Average American, spent more time watching TV than doing anything else except sleeping and working. No wonder so many people are agitating for a shorter work week. They need more time to watch TV.

Now get this. The surveys show that you actually **sleep less** each year in order to increase your daily TV fix. Is this what you want? Apparently.

Now let's look at the country as a whole. Fewer people are voting every year. Crime and divorce rates are climbing. American productivity is falling off. And if Scholastic Aptitude Test scores are any indication, people are actually getting stupider as the amount of time spent watching television steadily increases.

THE NINE COMMON DANGER SIGNS OF TV ADDICTION

1. Do you miss Walter Cronkite?
2. Do you wait faithfully, and fully expect to get "more at eleven"?
3. Does the first-grade teacher complain that your kid won't listen unless she dresses up like Big Bird?
4. Do you feel that you deserve a break today?
5. Do power blackouts give you the shakes?
6. Have you taken to wearing a bulletproof vest to avoid becoming another victim of random violence?
7. Are you ashamed to admit that you know who shot J.R.?
8. Do you always check the TV schedule before accepting party invitations?
9. Does your sex drive resurface when Johnny Carson goes on vacation?

So why do so many spend so much time with the tube? Perhaps it's just a habit. Some habits are good for you — like brushing your teeth or doing the laundry before you run out of underwear. But some habits are bad for you — like smoking or getting into debt with your credit cards. And when people can't stop doing something that is bad for them, then it's not a habit. It's an addiction.

TV-watching is an addiction that has reached epidemic proportions. And yet, most TV addicts are not even aware of their problem. This is despite the fact that the nine common danger signs are painfully familiar to the vast majority of Americans.

But what can you do about it? The cold-turkey treatment has been successful only with people who are willing to move to rural areas where the reception is so bad that you can't tell the difference between Barbara Walters and Dan Rather. TV critics have panned almost every show on the air since *Playhouse 90,* but people still keep watching. Some day genetic engineering will offer a permanent solution, but for now it's only a gleam in the scientists' eyes.

A cold look at these hard facts can be devastating. One man threw his brand-new Sony into the river when he dreamed that Ed McMahon was his father.

MY PERSONAL STRUGGLE WITH ADDICTION

But I know that TV addiction can be cured. I know because **I am an ex–TV addict.** Here is my story.

I once had a normal life: a wife, two kids, a 16 percent mortgage, and a white-collar job in the federal bureaucracy. I woke up to David Hartman's gleaming, toothy smile. I memorized the national weather map. Walter Cronkite came to dinner every night. I spent my evenings with Laverne and Hawkeye and Lou Grant and Benson. Weekends were made for Michelob and major sports events. I even liked Howard Cosell.

Sure, there were a few minor problems. Once the kids strapped a neighbor's boy into his Big Wheel and catapulted him across the freeway. They said it was really incredible.

But then things really began to fall apart. I didn't get the promotion I had been counting on. The guy who beat me out told me his secret. He had been reading *Time* magazine while I had been watching *The Love Boat.* I was crushed.

The last straw was the camping trip. My wife thought it would be a change of pace. She was tired of our annual pilgrimage to Burbank. And it *was* true that we hadn't once been selected for *Family Feud* in seven years of trying. So I agreed, reluctantly.

MY FAMILY BEFORE THE TRAGEDY

We marched into the wilderness for three straight days. I kept thinking about all the shows I was missing. The campsites looked like *Little House on the Prairie*. The park ranger looked like Trapper John. And the birds! Their incessant chirping reminded me of Dick Cavett. I thought I was going to explode!

Then we met that family of bears. The kids thought the cubs were the Muppets. The mother bear, who came charging down the hill, looked just like Morley Safer on assignment for *60 Minutes*. So naturally I went up to him expecting to be interviewed. As my wife tried to pull me away, I tripped on a rock and passed out. I guess that's what saved me.

People were very understanding. I even got on the national news. But only I knew the truth. TV addiction had wiped out my whole family.

In my despair, I leaned even harder on the tube. Finally, the boss walked in and caught me watching *All My Children* on a three-inch portable I had rigged up in the file cabinet. He fired me on the spot.

I moved myself and a twenty-five-inch Zenith into a seedy room on the edge of the city. I could feel my identity slowly dissolve into that big color screen. Sometimes I thought I was Barney Miller, sometimes Lucille Ball.

I finally decided to end my useless life and take the awful glowing nemesis with me. I put on my karate outfit and lunged at the screen. Then everything went black.

I woke up the next day in a hospital bed. The nurse told me a team of microsurgeons had worked all night to reattach my feet. The prognosis was good, but I'd be laid up for at least a month. She smiled as she lowered a spring-mounted TV in front of me and turned it on. *Hollywood Squares* was on. I fell asleep as Paul Lynde made a risqué comment on the mating habits of Labrador retrievers. The studio audience went wild.

I came to the next morning. Feeling rested, I resolved to find a way to kick the TV habit without incurring any more outrageous medical bills. I knew I could build a bridge back to human society. I decided to make friends with the hemorrhoid patient in the next bed. I glanced over. He was watching *The Price Is Right.*

I turned away and tried to make sense of my life. A social worker came in to ask why I had kicked in my TV set. Without thinking, I blurted out, "TV self-defense."

A dim primordial impulse welled up from deep within my subconscious. TV Self-Defense. I *would* find some way to stop watching TV. But how?

I knew that for the cure to work, it had to be as easy as turning on the set and as simple as changing the channel. The social worker gave me a deck of cards and left, her face ashen with despair. I don't know why, but something told me the answer was in the cards.

Interviewer: If you had to choose, would you rather give up watching TV forever, or talking to your father forever?

First child: Talking to my dad.
Second Child: It's hard. My dad.
Third Child: Give up TV forever.
Fourth child: Giving up my father.
Fifth Child: The TV forever.
Sixth child: Give up talking to my dad forever.

"TV or Not TV," *Bill Moyers' Journal,* April 23, 1979 (show no. 412, library no. M-12).

KIDS PICK TV OVER DAD

I spent two frustrating days experimenting. I taped the cards over the air inlets in the back of the set, hoping the thing would overheat and blow itself up. I stuck them onto the antenna, thinking that this would obscure the reception and make it easier not to watch. (I felt like Thomas Edison trying to invent the light bulb.) I even ate one.

Hollywood Squares gave me the answer. A shot of the whole playing board was on the screen. In a fit of pique, I taped a card over Paul Lynde's cubicle. Something snapped. He was gone. Then, in rapid succession, I covered up the rest of the panel. And then I turned off the set.

I knew that at long last I had found the cure to a problem that has so vexed mankind since 1946.

Since that fateful day, I have refined the system. Laboratory and field tests have proved its effectiveness. An editor whom I treated, himself so seriously afflicted that he could no longer read even Judith Krantz novels, finally convinced me to publish. "It could save the world," he said. "Not to mention my career."

If you're ready to take the first step on the road to TV independence, then keep reading. If not, then please pass this book on to someone else. Or better yet, convince him to buy his own copy.

A.2
The Process of TV Addiction: A Theory of Addictive Dynamics

I began my career as a TV-addiction-treatment specialist with an almost messianic sense of mission. The world was filled with hopeless victims crying out for help. I felt I had only to announce my cure to the public and they would beat a path to my door. Accordingly, I rented an office in a modern medical complex, placed a discreet ad in the paper, and waited for the results.

The ensuing weeks of morguelike stillness in my waiting room gave me some pause. Perhaps naive enthusiasm had led me astray. In a bold change of strategy, I went to the local shopping mall to hand out promotional brochures. There I learned the awful truth. People thought I was a kook to question their TV habits. Virtually no one would admit to such a basic disability, at least not in public.

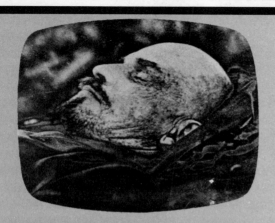

THE TOP TEN SOVIET TV SHOWS

1. Live from Lenin's Tomb
2. Leave It to Leonid
3. I Was a Dissident Judeo-Christian Writer for the KGB
4. Call-in Commissar
5. The Pope, His Many Wives and Children
6. Friendly Afghanistan: Scenic and Serene
7. How to Operate a Telephone
8. Bowling for Food Ration Cards
9. Prostitution in America: A Way of Life
10. Red Army Band Rehearsal — Live!

Humiliation drove me into the waiting arms of a marketing consultant. He told me in a half-hour and at great expense that I had a product identity problem not unlike the one that Jesus Christ had faced. I would have to educate the public about the nature and causes of TV addiction if I expected to get enough paying customers to turn my visionary concept into a solvent business. This, he guessed, would cost at least two million dollars.

Undaunted, I did what all men with great ideas and very little cash do. I formed a nonprofit corporation and had stationery printed up. Luckily, the secretary of state was looking for a cost-effective way to hypnotize the Warsaw pact nations. I reasoned that since American TV was clearly addictive here at home, perhaps it would have a similar effect on the Eastern bloc. My case was bolstered when I found a list of the top ten Soviet TV shows, which I knew had not caused a single minute of TV addiction in Russia's client states.

Three weeks after I submitted the proposal, "Television: A Cool Medium for a Cold War," I received a $750,000 grant to do a feasibility study for TV Free Europe. With my funding assured, I hired a stable of jobless Ph.D.s and began to review the literature. I quickly identified six major groups of TV addicts.

TYPE CBS   These people think that Walter Cronkite is God and that He sent Archie Bunker to Earth to make them laugh. They hold J. R. Ewing personally responsible for rising oil prices and they are grateful that Loni Anderson has given new meaning to the concept of pendulous development. They feel that Mike Wallace, if unleashed, is capable of eating his lapel mike on the air. They dream about going to war in an Asian country and having their wounds treated humorously but compassionately by Alan Alda.

TYPE NBC   These unfortunate souls do not think of people as real unless they smile a lot while looking into portable television cameras. They exhibit tremendous feelings of inferiority, always thinking that they'll be number three. They are sure that some day Gary Coleman will run for the U.S. Senate, and they have decided to vote for him. They think of Barbara Mandrell as the world's first bionic country singer. They think that Tom Brokaw's speech impediment is cute and that Johnny Carson owns most of Las Vegas. They miss Tom Snyder.

TYPE PBS Typically these people dress like Alistair Cooke and have fake English accents. They are capable of limited conversation on such topics as Pavarotti's shirt size but claim not to know who won the Super Bowl. They write checks for thirty-five dollars when they hear the sound of many telephones ringing. Unconsciously, they feel that Mr. Rogers is a hermaphrodite. You may run into a Type PBS who won't admit to watching any TV. He can be tricked into a full confession if you begin a flawed plot summary of *Upstairs, Downstairs*.

TYPE HBO These people own an average of .75 Betamaxes and buy an average of 28 blank video cassettes per year. They feel that seeing even a fleeting glimpse of full-frontal nudity in the privacy of their own homes is worth at least twenty dollars a month. They have memorized the entire Sean Connery role from *Doctor No.* Because they want to be the kind of people who don't miss out, twenty-four hours a day, they rarely fall completely asleep.

TYPE ABC   These people name their children Fonzie and Mork and always say "sports" when asked to complete the line, "wide world of _____." They have a deep-set, unquestioning belief in a philosophy best expressed by the phrase "That's incredible." They are beset by escapist fantasies about islands. They are sure that Charlie's Angels have all gone to heaven, and they hope fervently that Ted Koppel will stop talking through his teeth at people who appear before him on giant TV screens at eleven-thirty at night.

TYPE KID   These people will watch anything.

THE PERILS OF PROXIMITY, I

THE LAWS OF PROXIMITY

The publication of the six addict profiles in an elite academic journal brought unanimous praise from my learned peers in the social sciences. But I was concerned that they might not be universally understood. I knew the average addict felt that "relief" was spelled R–O–L–A–I–D–S. I needed something that would look good in block letters.

With this in mind, and after a prolonged period of daydreaming, I began to work on a coherent theory of addictive dynamics. A blinding flash of sheer intuition yielded the **First Law of Proximity:**

> **People almost always watch TV when they are close to a working set and without something else that absolutely must be done which needs their sense of vision.**

When a favorite niece reported a close encounter with a bread knife at the hands of her addicted mother, I produced the **First Law of Proximity (revised):**

> **People almost always watch TV when they are close to a working set.**

The pristine elegance of this formulation set the entire research staff agog, but I still wasn't satisfied. I felt it was a bit too wordy. And so I struck out again for the shopping mall, where I knew the man on the street now resided. I had barely penetrated the mazelike parking complex before I found my solution.

A motley band of teen-agers was navigating a late-model luxury sedan through the lot's outer rings at about a hundred miles per hour. (I later learned they were members of a merciless gang that preyed on mall patrons who had lost track of their parking spots.) Distracted by a security-force vehicle in hot pursuit, they mistook an expressway exit ramp for a safe channel of escape and fused the front end of their auto onto the bumper of an oncoming concrete mixer.

I approached the car to offer assistance. To my amazement, I found (in addition to three comatose bodies) a small portable TV set still dangling from the rearview mirror. They had been watching *CHiPs.*

This scene impacted on me like a federal budget cutback. Before me was a new, hybrid form of proto-addict, unlimited by the traditional need for alternating current. I had to expand the scope of the Proximity Theory to include these battery people, to whom TV was obviously more important than life itself.

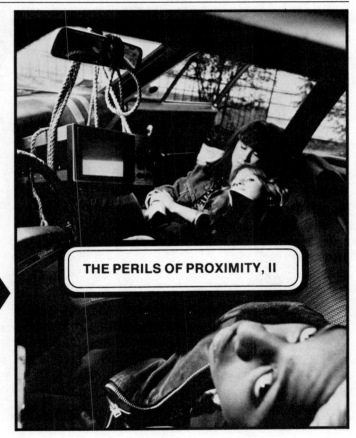

THE PERILS OF PROXIMITY, II

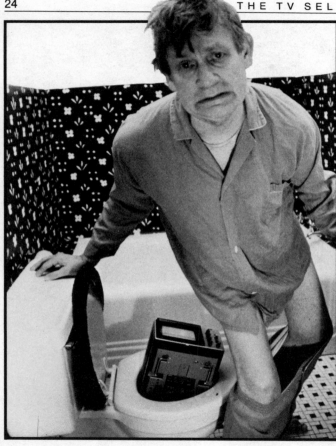

And thus was born the **Second Law of Proximity:**

Where man goes, TV cannot be far behind.

“[In the year 2029] shopping will be done by TV. Customers will have hookups to stores, which will allow them to see and buy merchandise in the comfort of their own homes. The TV will not be an appliance as we know it today. TV will be designed into people's homes in all the rooms. Including the john.”

Joe Lamneck, Director of TV Production, Norman Craig & Kummel, "Ad Makers View the Future, Mad Avenue: 2029," *Back Stage*, June 22, 1979.

WHITHER THOU GOEST, TV WILL FOLLOW.

A horrid dream inspired the **Third Law of Proximity:**

> **One man, one TV set, one heck of a lousy world.**

I AM IN THE CITY. I APPROACH A [...] *IS SO DOWNCAST. WHAT HE IS LOOK-GRIFFIN SHOW ON HANGS FROM HIS HIDEOUS ELECTRONIC ALBATROSS.*

EVERYONE LOOKS SAD. MAN TO ASK WHY HE AND THEN I SEE ING AT: THE MERV A TINY TV THAT NECK LIKE SOME

66 The arrival of new video technology in the next decade will enable users to 'drop out of this society,' according to Jerry Astor, video marketing director of Akai America. He predicts that with advances in present-day techniques of gaming or simulation, 'we might be able to offer the individual the ultimate dream machine,' allowing the user to reproduce the characteristics of individuals in a computer — a kind of high-tech cloning. 99

"Solid State Technology Looming Large in Homevideo: Sez Akai Exec," *Variety,* December 2, 1981.

YES, BUT WHAT WILL IT COST?

THE LAWS OF BOREDOMONICS

Upon completion of the Proximity Theory, I turned my attention to the final question: WHY do people get hooked on TV? I knew that great thinkers, from Aristotle to Eric Sevareid, had grappled with issues like these without once producing an answer that could be expressed in a simple sentence. Undaunted, I made a comprehensive list of the possible causes.

- Is TV addiction caused by a massive mutation in the structure of human cells? Or is it merely a coincidence that the first atom bomb was detonated only a year before TV was introduced on a grand scale?

- Is it the inevitable result of a free-market economy that forces innocent multinational corporations to exploit the most cost-effective advertising medium known to man — regardless of the social consequences?

- Was it preordained by a greater being — call it God or an alien life-force — that we should suffer in a purgatory of wasted time and human potential — perhaps as a lesson, perhaps as a punishment? And would He, She, or It be willing to negotiate?

No! came the resounding answer from my brain. People watch TV because they're bored silly. And thus, the **First Law of Boredomonics:**

> **Watching TV is doing nothing while seeming to do something.**

At this point I called in my secretary and showed him my discovery. He read it and said, "Yeah. TV is a big waste of time. But everybody does it. So what?" This response provoked a catharsis in my thinking that led me to the **Second Law of Boredomonics:**

> **People watch TV because it's a socially accepted way to waste a lot of time.**

A potential threat to the logic of Boredomonics developed subsequently when my secretary accused me of wasting a lot of time without watching any TV whatsoever. I narrowly evaded a confrontation by showing the subtle distinction between **doing nothing creatively** (an activity to which I had become quite attached) and **doing nothing at all** (a mind set that leads inevitably to the heartbreak of TV addiction).

DOING NOTHING CREATIVELY

DOING NOTHING AT ALL

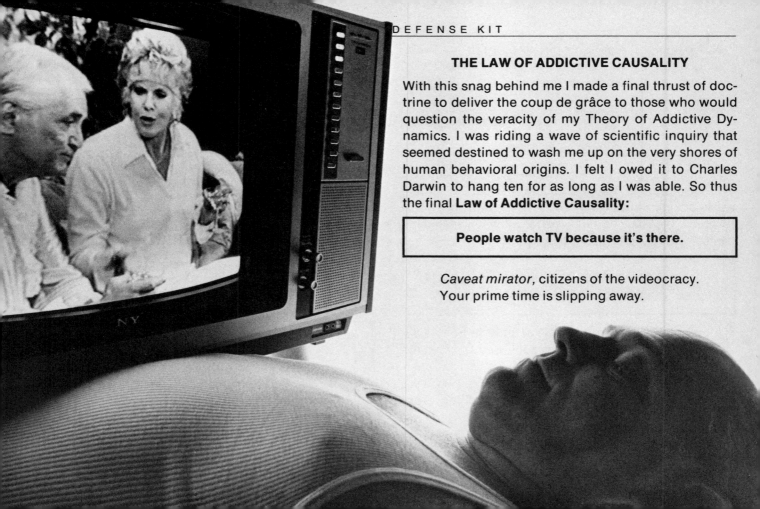

THE LAW OF ADDICTIVE CAUSALITY

With this snag behind me I made a final thrust of doctrine to deliver the coup de grâce to those who would question the veracity of my Theory of Addictive Dynamics. I was riding a wave of scientific inquiry that seemed destined to wash me up on the very shores of human behavioral origins. I felt I owed it to Charles Darwin to hang ten for as long as I was able. So thus the final **Law of Addictive Causality:**

> **People watch TV because it's there.**

Caveat mirator, citizens of the videocracy. Your prime time is slipping away.

A.3
The Effects: Six Specific Diseases Caused by TV

When I treat TV addicts I always administer the Home Entertainment History Analysis Test (HEHAT) during the intake interview. This often provokes the patient to recount tales of the most embarrassing depravity while he or she was in the TV-altered state.

Over time, certain patterns emerged from this mountain of transcripts. While cleaning up the office one day, I decided to analyze this evidence systematically so I could throw out all that paper and make space for another treatment room. Eight months and three microcomputers later I had generated the following list.

If you do not recognize yourself in one or more of the following pages, then you are probably either legally blind or have just arrived here from another planet. Welcome. In either case, I suggest a complete medical examination without delay.

Ted Koppel: We live in an era of great interpersonal loneliness that exists in this country, and television in many cases has become a surrogate.

David Brinkley: I got a letter the other day from an older lady who said she had had more conversation from me over all these years than she'd ever had from anyone else, which I thought was terribly sad, but nevertheless a fact.

"Television Journalists: Part 1," *The Dick Cavett Show*, WNET-TV, November 2, 1981 (show no. 5011).

NEWSMEN PEG TV AS LONELY HEARTS CLUB.

FOOTBALL DETACHMENT, CHRONIC

Chronic Football Detachment is marked by the almost complete emotional dissociation of male and female members of the family during weekend afternoons in the fall. It is thought to be the key factor in the alarming rise of multi-year subscriptions to *Ms*.

Behavior codes during this time are carefully prescribed and scrupulously followed under threat of divorce: The men drink life-threatening quantities of beer. During breaks in the action they give detailed but garbled renditions of alternative plays that could have been more prudently chosen to effect total annihilation of the cursed enemy. Toward the end of the fourth quarter, teeth chattering, high-decibel wailing, and body spasms are commonly observed, especially if the home team is losing.

It is the duty of the wife to offer relief to her afflicted partner without disturbing his transcendent stream of consciousness. This involves prearranged responses to short commands: "More brewski." "Chips now." "Bedpan." And so on.

Boys wear twenty-five-dollar football jerseys and expect the same treatment their fathers get. Girls, if they haven't yet run away, slip upstairs and fantasize about the private parts of the chemistry teacher.

COMMERCIALITIS, ACUTE INFECTIOUS

Clearly the most widespread form of addictive disease, Acute Infectious Commercialitis has often been compared with the new penicillin-resistant strains of gonorrhea. A distinct flattening of the wallet and the most grotesque deformation of the bank statement are almost always seen in such cases.

To determine if you are a victim, just answer the following questions, yes or no, without lying.

1. Do you find it difficult to have a Coke without smiling?
2. Do you feel you simply can't do it like McDonald's can?
3. Do you love New York, really?
4. In elevators and other public places, do you have an irresistible and almost compulsive desire to reach out and touch someone?
5. Did you pay more than $28.50 for your jeans?
6. Do you feel cocky and defiant because you beat the greasies?
7. Can you relieve yourself without squeezing the toilet tissue?
8. The last time you went shopping for a car, was it just one look? Was that all it took?
9. Would you like to be a Pepper, too?

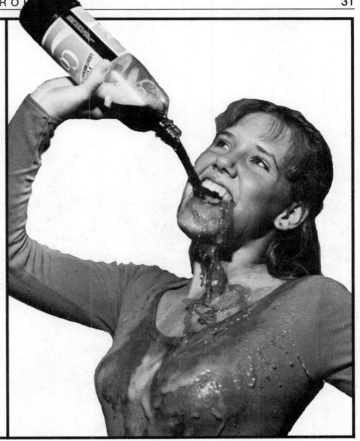

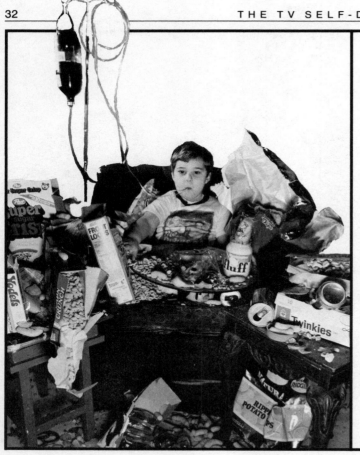

CARTOONOSIS, POLYTROPHIC

Polytrophic Cartoonosis is marked by the progressive degeneration of a child's musculature until the parents are called in to change the channel from *The Bugs Bunny Show* to *Superfriends* to *Smurfs,* and so on. Parents often unwittingly foster this variant by stocking the family larder with unlimited quantities of Cap'n Crunch, Twinkies, Miracle Whip, and Coke. These patients inevitably develop three to ten inches of fat in place of the muscles and completely lose sight of their feet.

Many parents were relieved when educational TV began programming *Sesame Street, Mr. Rogers,* and *Villa Alegre* on Saturday morning. But I ask you: What good is it that your kid can read and count to one hundred in English and Spanish if his nursery-school teacher repeatedly mistakes him for a quarter-scale model of the Goodyear blimp?

HYPERGAMESHOWITIS

Hypergameshowitis is usually seen in women. Lately, however, it has spread to unemployed auto workers of both sexes and to a new species, discovered by Phil Donahue, called the house husband.

The symptoms are not only embarrassing but can lead to serious injury if untreated. If you have ever considered, or actually exhibited, the following behavior, you are a victim.

While standing in the major-appliance section of the local Sears, you suddenly start jumping up and down, squealing, and clapping your hands. The salesman thinks that someone put a lizard in your underpants, but actually you're waiting for him to say, "Carol Molinaro — COME ON DOWN!" When nobody offers you either two hundred dollars in cash or what's behind the screen, you grab a crisper drawer out of the nearest Frigidaire, put it on your head, and demand to see Monty Hall.

MALDEN'S PARANOIA

Sufferers of Malden's Paranoia have given the American tourist a bad reputation at home and abroad. This is because American Express traveler's checks have replaced the crucifix as the preferred tool of exorcism for today's Dracula surrogate, the mugger.

Overwhelmed by a frenzy of fear induced nightly by televised scenes of victimization at the hands of unseen yet ever present villains, the common man has dispensed with logic when contemplating any travel beyond the secure perimeter of his front yard. Symptoms include:

- A worrisome rise in the number of unprovoked Macings of dark-skinned, subteen males.
- A tendency of Americans to move about foreign cities in defensive formations approved by the Green Berets.
- An unnatural, somewhat childlike dependence on minor authority figures such as train conductors, hotel desk clerks, and Laundromat attendents.
- A complete inability to leave home without it.

JIGGLISM, SPASMODIC (T & A STRAINS)

Spasmodic Jigglism is a clear example of "better living through chemistry." TV producers willing to exploit the new textile technology have filled the screen with two specific portions of the young female anatomy, which are then placed in rapid motion and restrained only by thin but powerful pieces of modern synthetic fabric.

Severe neck pain often occurs when older males attempt to track the body parts in question during sequences of jogging, rope jumping, and trampoline exercise. Recent widespread use of slow-motion photography, however, has dramatically reduced these complaints.

The most pathetic victims of Jigglism are twelve- to fourteen-year-old males. Look for a marked increase in the frequency and duration of visits to the least conspicuous bathroom in the house. Less mentally adept boys may try in vain to look down Morgan Fairchild's flouncy, low-cut patio dress by standing directly over the screen.

More surprising is the high rate of Jigglism among females. Common signs are Sis dressing as a two-dollar whore and Mom prancing about during *The Tonight Show* in a Frederick's of Hollywood outfit.

TV DINNERS

"Forty-five percent of all Americans eat dinner with the television on . . . Dinnertime used to be the family time for talk . . . [With the TV on] you can still talk, but you're talking about something outside your own family that's brought in; you are communing in the presence of a great corporate religion coming in through a pulpit that is in every home, with tireless messengers sending out centralized messages; and that makes the experience and the common basis of discourse for most people a kind of wholesale product."

—Dr. George Gerbner, dean,
Annenberg School of Communications,
University of Pennsylvania

"In day-to-day commerce, television is not so much interested in the business of communications as in the business of delivering people to the advertisers. *People* are the merchandise, not the shows. The shows are merely the bait.

"The consumer, whom the custodians of the medium are pledged to serve, is in fact served up."

—Les Brown,
Television: The Business Behind the Box

"With TV, the viewer is the screen."
—Marshall McLuhan

TVSDK

B. THE SOLUTION

THE TV SELF-DEFENSE
TREATMENT MANUAL

You have reached a most delicate point in your psychic life. You have been forced to admit the unthinkable: **you are now, and have always been, a hopeless TV addict.**

You have wasted literally tens of thousands of hours in your life so far. Yet, despite your guilt and self-loathing, you seem unable to turn the wretched tube off. You watch just one more show — then another and another, until it's way past your bedtime.

Locked in an endless cycle of addiction, you have become obsessed by a desire to die and be reborn as a Hawaiian Punch flavor crystal. You are at the end of your rope.

But look at it this way: You are in just the right state of mind to undertake the TVSDK regimen! The following **Treatment Manual** begins with a short explanation of the theory behind the system. Putting this theory into practice, you will master a technique that will free you from a lifetime of crippling dependence. Have faith! The dawn is about to break on this, your darkest hour. You can bet your bottom dollar on it.

SONY

B.1
The Theory of TVSDK

At the heart of the TVSDK treatment package is a concept called **distancing.** It is not used in training for the Boston Marathon.

Distancing was invented by Bertolt Brecht, an unruly German playwright who shocked and amused and enraged and bored audiences during the first half of the twentieth century. A lifelong Communist, he also wrote the words to "Mack the Knife," one of Bobby Darin's favorite songs.

Brecht was a man with a problem. Writing during Hitler's rise to power, he wanted to make people sit up and think about the political trends that were about to engulf them. But when he looked out at the traditional theater audience, he saw "motionless bodies in a curious state — they seem . . . to have relaxed after violent strain . . . They have their eyes open but they don't look, they stare . . . as if spellbound."

Such an entranced audience, he reasoned, would not perceive any social message in the play. They were asleep at the wheel.

He finally hit upon the idea of distancing — consciously keeping the audience from emotional involvement in the drama. He used such radical techniques as putting the end at the beginning and the actors in the audience. This was supposed to prevent spectators from being sucked into the theatrical illusion.

Unfortunately for Brecht, things did not work out as planned. As often as not, the patrons were distanced so much by his work that they failed to take their seats before the performance — or even buy tickets. ➤

TYPICAL BRECHTIAN AUDIENCE

But luckily, you can now benefit from this principle of distancing. The exercises that follow, like Brecht's theater tricks, will push you away from TV, a medium you have come to take for granted. As you step back and observe your TV-abuse patterns, you will be repulsed by what you see. Finally, you will succeed in alienating yourself completely from this illusionary medium. And then you will turn the set off for good.

You may wonder how you will be able to track the progress of your TV distancing. For the answer, I turn to the world's undisputed heavyweight-champion media guru, the late Marshall McLuhan. During the sixties he had a way of saying things that seemed to jump out of his mouth directly onto the pages of almost every popular magazine. His words, especially in short takes, looked great in print, even though nobody really understood them. Not bad for an English professor. McLuhan divided all forms of human communication into hot and cool media. Hot media, like print, he said, do not demand much participation on the part of the receiver. Cool media, like TV, call for a great deal.

But many people find it difficult to classify a toddler watching "Wheelie and the Chopper Bunch" as "involved." McLuhan clarified his thoughts in *Understanding Media,* noting "a paradoxical feature of the 'cool' TV medium. It involves us in moving depth, but it does not excite, agitate, or arouse." TV, it seems, involves us like heroin.

To give a modest homage to the unquestioned brilliance of his work, I have updated McLuhan's findings. The Haller All-Purpose Media Analysis Temperature Scale (HAPMAT Scale) measures a person's *reaction* to a medium rather than the medium itself.

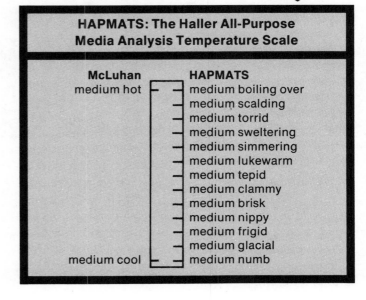

HAPMATS: The Haller All-Purpose Media Analysis Temperature Scale

McLuhan	HAPMATS
medium hot	medium boiling over
	medium scalding
	medium torrid
	medium sweltering
	medium simmering
	medium lukewarm
	medium tepid
	medium clammy
	medium brisk
	medium nippy
	medium frigid
	medium glacial
medium cool	medium numb

TYPICAL HAPMATS PROGRESSION:

Boiling Over

Torrid

Lukewarm

Numb

The real purpose of HAPMATS is to describe one's reaction to, and therefore distance from, the medium of TV. Since you are now a confirmed addict, your mental response to the TV experience will be on the cool end of the scale (numb, glacial, or frigid). As you advance through the TVSDK treatment and your brain slowly begins to reactivate, you will find yourself bumping up through the middle range (clammy, tepid, and lukewarm).

As you reach the final stage of cathartic rage at your TV involvement, you will naturally gravitate toward the upper range (sweltering, torrid, scalding) until you hit the acme of media temperature, boiling over.

Rate yourself frequently during the following exercises. It will get your mind off the terror you will feel when you realize what you have gotten yourself into.

THE QUESTION OF COLD TURKEY

I am often asked, "What about going cold turkey? Why not just make up your mind, go into the living room, unplug the set and then call the Salvation Army to come pick it up?"

The simple answer is that it doesn't work. You must develop an almost visceral contempt for the medium. Try to approximate the feeling that the Ayatollah Khomeini had for the Shah of Iran.

This takes time. You must fully experience each emotion on the HAPMAT Scale, gradually nurturing an unshakable sense of outrage within your soul. Premature rejection of the offensive object will inevitably lead to intense pangs of remorse followed by a blind, high-speed race to the nearest appliance store for the purchase of personal portables for everyone in the family.

Let me assure you that I fully understand the difficulty with which Americans approach any task that cannot be conceived and accomplished in less than three minutes. But you must think of the TVSDK program as a meditation, an almost Oriental process that, while denying you the cheap thrills of immediate gratification, will ultimately lead to an inner strength equal to the task at hand. Trust me.

B.2
Preparatory Exercises

The three sets of preparatory exercises — **TV Graffiti, Symbolic Deployment,** and **Psyching Up** — will help you ascend the HAPMAT Scale. For this you will need to collect certain items.

If you are, or have, a child, these materials are probably nearby. Otherwise, make a quick trip to a local art-supply store and purchase them. Remember: With these materials and the TVSDK you will buy more time in your life, something of incalculable value. So don't be cheap.

Now remove everything from the top of your TV set — you will eventually have to find another place for these knickknacks anyway. This will be your **TVSDK Work Station.** You needn't place a protective coating of newspaper here. The more gouges you have in the set, the less likely you are to keep it around the house after the project is finished.

1. Roll of heavy-duty clear plastic food wrap
2. Scissors and knife
3. Assorted felt-tip pens
4. Pack of single-edge razors *or* X-Acto Knife
5. Roll of quality, double-stick adhesive tape
6. Fire axe
7. Assortment of colored construction paper

Not Shown: Yardstick or measuring tape
Note: The white paper atop the set is for display purposes only. You won't be needing this. See text.

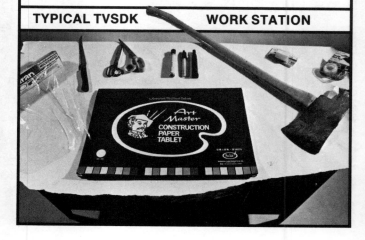

TYPICAL TVSDK   WORK STATION

Do not concern yourself with the resale value of the set. **Resale of TV sets is a mortal sin.** Your goal is to humiliate the set, not worship it. You might as well start right now.

Before beginning the actual exercises, you should establish a beachhead on your screen without delay. In the unlikely event that the set is off, turn it on. Cut out a piece of black paper of at least six square inches (2" × 3" will do just fine). Apply the double-stick tape to one side and mount it on the face of the screen. ➡

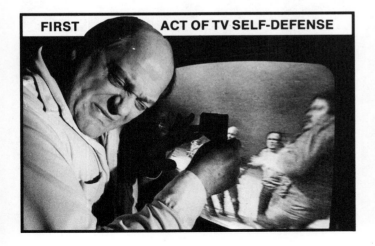

FIRST　　ACT OF TV SELF-DEFENSE

Stand back and survey your work. Your eyes will be drawn to the perky little black anomaly. Your mind will begin to think independently for the first time since 1946 or your birth, whichever is more recent. Thoughts like "Gleem fights the enemies of your mouth" will mysteriously vanish from your memory cells.

In the black hole of primal TV blockage, you will sense a glimmer of personal freedom unlike anything you have ever experienced. You will momentarily register perhaps a simmering on the HAPMAT Scale. Thousands of hours of video enslavement will flash before your eyes.

Then you will begin to feel nauseated. You will think, "Who told me to buy this book, anyway? This will never work." You will instinctively look around the room to see if anyone has been watching you.

Quickly counteract this sense of revulsion. An excellent tactic is to rush out to the nearest bookstore and buy ten more copies of the TVSDK. When you return, hand out copies to all present.

Stack the remaining gift copies on top of the set. This will greatly improve your chances of being classified as part of a cultural revolution rather than just another oddball crackpot who enjoys molesting the fruits of an advanced technological society.

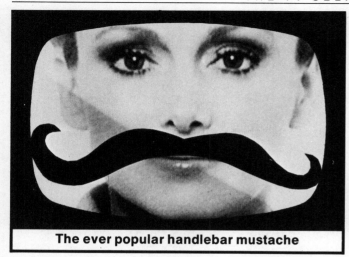

The ever popular handlebar mustache

Punk-rock sunglasses for Walter Cronkite

TV GRAFFITI

Graffiti occupies an honored place in the annals of human self-expression. It is the voice of the common man, a forum for inner longings that must be expressed without stylistic restraint or censorship. Its canvas is the most intimate surface of the human habitat, like public toilet stalls and subway cars. Its tools are the crude instruments at hand, like felt-tip pens and spray paint. It is the repository of the wit and wisdom of men and women barred from the traditional channels of communication by an accident of birth, a subversive instinct, or a natural inability to spell.

TV Graffiti will enable you to subvert the intended meaning of the TV images. It will begin the distancing process in an atmosphere of playfulness. It will ward off those suicidal impulses that may creep into your mind as you contemplate a life without TV. It will help you think of the TVSDK as your friend, not an impersonal barrier between you and your only current

Pinocchio nose for Larry Hagman

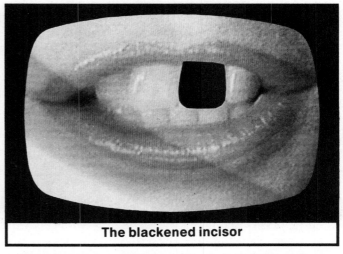

The blackened incisor

source of solace. It will permit you to talk back to your TV in an interactive, creative way and foster a sense of power over a seemingly impassive and impenetrable medium. And besides, it's a hell of a party game.

To begin, do whatever is necessary to put yourself back into an elementary-school state of mind. Now select a program that has a recurring close-up of the human face and a somewhat stodgy tone. Suggestions are the evening news, Alistair Cooke's introduction to *Masterpiece Theatre,* and presidential addresses.

Select an appropriate appliqué design from the accompanying photographs, cut it out of your black paper, and apply the double-stick tape. Approach the TV set and wait for the close-up. Then strike, at the most embarrassing place you can imagine.

If the results do not render you silly, then you can be sure the humor receptors in your brain have been deadened by laugh-track overexposure. The only legal remedy for this is to get a child to play the game with you. If that doesn't work, find a funnier child.

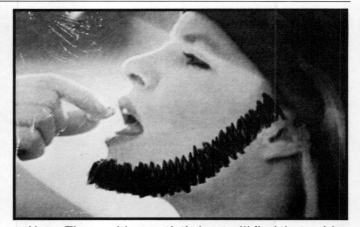

Another way to play TV Graffiti is to draw directly on the screen. First, tear off enough Saran Wrap to completely cover it up. Stretch it across the tube and let go. Voilà! It will stick as though the screen were a bowl of leftover egg salad. Select a target image that you would like to defile. Then simply attack it with your felt-tip pen when it appears for more than a few seconds.

Goofy improvisation is the watchword of TV Graffiti. Plumb the depths of your unconscious. Let your fantasies run wild. Use additional materials at will. I can only hint at the possibilities, because of the publisher's desire to offend no living potential book buyer.

Note: Those with an artistic bent will find that a video tape recorder with a freeze frame is a handy tool for doing more detailed works of TV Graffiti. The freeze frame can isolate a single frame (a thirtieth of a second) of even the fastest moving commercial. Then, you can react to it at your leisure and carefully express your rage in felt-tip and Saran Wrap.

I'd love to see the results of your experiments with this technique. Send photos of your work on the screen to the address listed on page 80. The best camera setting is f4-5.6 at 1/30 second using 400 ASA film.

SYMBOLIC DEPLOYMENT

We live in a polyglot society. As the global village shrinks, people who do not share the same language often have to share the same public facilities. Graphic designers have responded to this trend by putting up universal symbols wherever they can. This means everyone knows where and when they can do what without asking.

Symbolic deployment is a custom-made version of this universal language. Use it to send specific messages to yourself or other members of your household about shows that are high on your hit list. Some of the codes have general applications as well. In any case, you can communicate without having to talk very much, something at which the typical addict is not normally adept.

As with TV Graffiti, you can fabricate the symbols from construction paper or draw them directly over the screen on Saran Wrap. Again, don't be afraid to use your imagination to create additional symbols as needed.

UNIVERSAL NO-NO SIGN

Same as the sign on the cover of this book. Everyone understands this one. Make it from red construction paper. Place it on the set at night and see what effect it has on *The Today Show.*

LEFT/RIGHT TURN AHEAD

For shows that evidence a clear political point of view.

X-RATED

Like the motion-picture rating symbol. Those sensitive to sexual exploitation will find many uses for this one. A variation: Partially block out that part of the screen in which the offensive organs appear. Great for neglected wives of Type HBOs.

ALMIGHTY-DOLLAR SIGN

Could apply to any commercial TV show. Best for ads. A sage observer of the TV scene once remarked that having an FCC license to broadcast commercial television signals is like having a license to print money.

WARNING: RADIATION

Will remind you that when you watch TV you are looking down the barrel of a 25,000-volt, electron-beam gun. Also good for addresses by heads of superpower states.

PSYCHING-UP EXERCISES

This is the penultimate step in the TVSDK process. Distancing will take on an almost tangible meaning during the Psyching-up Exercises.

You will place both the object and the experience of TV in several new physical and emotional contexts. This will help you stop thinking of it as just another innocent home appliance. Remember, very few people waste 90 percent of their free time making toast.

At times you may feel like a Moonie who is being deprogrammed. This is perfectly apt. You have abdicated your personal autonomy to the cult of television. Now you must regain control of your mind — by force when necessary.

INVERSION

Turn your TV upside-down and watch. Wonder how Richard Simmons can dance, sing, and act like a four-year-old while stuck to the studio ceiling. Turn the TV on its side and watch George Jefferson enter his apartment through the ceiling door and walk down the wall.

MULTIPLES

Put all your TVs in one spot. Tune them all to Barbara Walters and wonder why she likes to talk to herself so much. Multiple cacophony: Switch each TV to a different channel. Multiple inversion: Make your own TV mandala as shown above. Synesthetic multiples: Watch one show's picture and listen to another's sound (or the radio or a record).

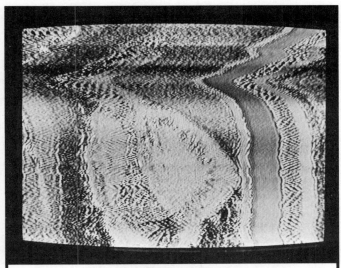

PSYCHEDELIA

Distort the image by detuning it. Wonder why the weather map looks like the pulsating cosmic beyond. If you want to relive the sixties, do multiple-set psychedelia.

SCREAMING EXERCISE

Pick a TV turn-off time. Set your alarm clock. When it rings, open your mouth and begin screaming at the top of your lungs. Continue shrieking as you get out of your chair, approach the set, bend over, and turn it off. An excellent way to go to bed before three o'clock in the morning.

SILENCE DRILLS

Turn the set off with a Screaming Exercise. Sit down and listen. Your mind will race to fill the void with reruns of *Gunsmoke*. Focus on a neutral object. Relax and let your mind wander. Ponder the Theory of Boredomonics. Try to do nothing creatively.

If you have conscientiously carried out the Psyching-up Exercises, you will now feel somewhat light-headed. You will laugh inappropriately. You will pace up and down the living room like a caged animal about to be fed. Your feelings will oscillate between ecstasy and melancholy.

One day you will have an almost irresistible urge to fling the TV set through the picture window. The next day you will want to watch all twenty-nine episodes of *My Mother the Car* back to back.

This is a reflection of your inner life. It is the product of a still-enslaved mind locked in mortal combat with itself. Freedom beckons like a *Playboy* centerfold. You just can't get your hands on it.

Try to calm down. Schedule extra visits with your psychiatrist. Invent a mantra like "No TV will make me free," and repeat it endlessly when you feel overwhelmed. Eat from the four basic food groups and be sure to get plenty of rest. You will need to muster all your strength for the battle you are about to fight.

BACKSLIDING
These rare photographs illustrate a common, though normally private, crisis in those who brave the rigors of TV Self-Defense: backsliding. This man had not been in a room with a working TV set for over twenty years. And yet at the close of a grueling modeling session, during which he graciously demonstrated the proper techniques for the Screaming Exercise and Silence Drill (see facing page), he was overcome by an irresistible urge to watch *Queen for a Day* "just one more time!" I didn't have the heart to tell him it was canceled in 1964.

B.3
Now Do It!

This is the moment you have been waiting for. The months, perhaps years, of exhausting preparatory exercises are over. You are ready for the final countdown to TV freedom. The process is deceptively simple:

You will apply the TVSDKards to your TV screen on a one-a-day schedule until you have totally bricked it up. Then you will turn off the set, and read the last part of this book, which will explain what to do with all your free time.

Ready? Take a HAPMATS reading. Boiling over? Then begin. Turn to page 82 and follow the instructions for removing the TVSDKards from the book. Note: This part involves the use of sharp instruments. Concentrate on this task as if you were handling live ammo. Surging emotions will cause your hands to tremble with anticipation. So **be careful.** Keep the ultimate goal in mind and your hand steady on the razor.

Inspect the Kards. Handle them lovingly — they are your key to a new life. Printed on each Kard is the TVSDK logo. This has several purposes. It will help you orient the Kards properly (horizontally). It will drill into your mind the ultimate purpose of the Kards — **TV Self-Defense.** And it will remind you to keep your TVSDK gift supply well stocked in case still-addicted friends drop by unexpectedly.

Note: The following procedures require knowledge of rudimentary math concepts. If you need help, consult either with someone in the sixth grade or with a home computer.

KARD DEPLOYMENT FORMULA (KDF)

Each Kard has the same height-to-width ratio (3:4) as a TV screen. Thus,

$$\frac{2\frac{1}{4}''}{3''} \text{ (Kard dimensions)} = \frac{3}{4} = \frac{\text{height}}{\text{width}} \text{ ratio of any TV.}$$

This means that it will take the same number of horizontal and vertical rows to cover up your screen. Study the picture below and you'll see what I mean.

Screen Size	Under 5″	7-9″	10-13″	15-17″	19-21″
Total Kard no. (K_n)	1K	4K	9K	16K	25K
Row no. (K_r)	1R	2R	3R	4R	5R

Screen Size	23-25″	27″	30″	Over 30″	
Total Kard no. (K_n)	36K	49K	64K	(consider joining est)	
Row no. (K_r)	6R	7R	8R		

To determine how many Kards you'll need to cover up your TV, first determine the diagonal screen size. Now find your screen size on the chart above and read off the total Kard number (K_n) and the number of rows (K_r). If your screen is larger than 21 inches you will need more than the thirty Kards provided in the book. You can either make these extras up out of your black construction paper or cut them out of a gift copy.

Still confused? Then simply space out the Kards evenly on your screen and count them. This is K_n.

KARD DEPLOYMENT SCHEDULE (KDS)

Make up a Kard Deployment Schedule (KDS) like the one below. Here you will list the starting date and $K_n - 1$ consecutive days following it. Remember, a Kard a day keeps the TV away. Select a starting date that will maximize your chances for success. The summertime is by far the best season to begin. The screen will be filled with reruns, rejected pilots for series, and boring documentaries. Leave plenty of extra spaces below your projected final day to accommodate your inevitable backsliding. ➡️

I think I can do it. I'm totally prepared mentally. This will be truly fulfilling. 3	8 4-9-83 5 KARDS DESTROYED WHILE SEARCHING FOR CHARO'S CLEAVAGE.
No problem whatsoever. 3	9 4-10-83 JUST JOHNNY'S MONOLOG PLEASE! Why me?
Going with the flow— 83	10 4-11-83 I CAN'T STAND IT!
PLEASE, GOD 83	11 4-12-83 Piece of cake, except for brief interlude fixating on Mr. Rogers' sneaker visible in left corner.
CHEWED OFF 1 KARD. CLOSE CALL WITH PORTION LODGED IN THROAT. TEACH MARGE & KIDS HEIMLICH MANEUVER. -83	12 4-13-83 Must sleep in cradle again tonight.
OK. -83	13 4-14-83 CUT WRISTS WITH KARD EDGE IN PATHETIC SUICIDE GESTURE. HELP ME!
	I must conquer this hideous affliction. Figure out how many ... into compactor and ...

Try to plan diversionary activities following completion of the Total Blockage Sequence (TBS). A month-long camel trek across the Sahara will ensure total TV abstinence during the difficult postblockage days. If you have managed to reproduce, send the kids to a wilderness ego school like Outward Bound.

Collect your thoughts with the following exercise:

Begin a silence drill. Imagine a TV-free future. Example: You'll read the great books of antiquity in their original languages. An honorary MBA from Harvard will be sent to you by mail. You'll accept an upper-level management position in a socially conscious but highly profitable alternative-technology company in Aspen, Colorado. You'll take extended, paid, winter vacations in the Rockies, teaching migrant workers how to ski. Summers will be spent entertaining customers on your sixty-one-foot yawl somewhere off Nantucket. Members of the opposite sex will find you irresistible, but you will remain faithful to your spouse, a leading spokesperson for the National Audubon Society. Your child will discover a basic flaw in the proof of the isosceles triangle and be accepted by M.I.T. at the age of thirteen. She will go on to become the first third-party candidate to be elected President of the United States.

TOTAL BLOCKAGE SEQUENCE (TBS)

Reserve a specific time of the day for the Kard-placement ritual. Create a quasi-religious ceremony for this event. Incense, costumes, primitive chanting, and dancing are all acceptable options. Remember, there are certain high-risk hours for alcoholics (cocktail parties), ex-smokers (morning coffee, after meals), and ex—drug addicts (during Cheech & Chong movies). Take this into account when you select your time.

Start in the lower left-hand corner of the screen. Work your way across until you reach the end of the row. Then go to the row above and continue.

When you reach the final row of Kards, you may experience a somewhat ticklish problem: overconfidence. The ancient Greeks had a wonderful name for this concept: hubris. This describes a man whose pride makes him emulate the gods' behavior. This inevitably resulted in retribution from the gods who didn't like their space invaded. Remember Icarus? Don't try it. Stick to the schedule.

Overleaf:
Actual lab tests show how TVSDK works.

TYPICAL CARD PLACEMENT RITUAL

BEFORE TVSDK
Once considered a hopeless case, this man had not changed his facial expression noticeably since 1946.

TVSDK: Day 1
The results are immediate and dramatic. The critical mind awakens from its video trance.

TVSDK: Day 3
Partial blockage enables the subject to take Richard Simmons's vanity plate as a personal insult. Good progress.

TVSDK: Day 5
For the first time in his life, the subject realizes that he neither wants nor needs to know all about Princess Di's love secrets.

TVSDK: Day 10
Transient regression. A piercing, hypnotic gaze by David Hartman has brought the subject to his knees. He ponders suicide.

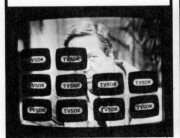

TVSDK: Day 12
Catharsis! Self-loathing has been totally converted into TV-directed cleansing rage.

TVSDK: Day 15
The end is near. The subject practices reaching for the on—off button. Nice use of Screaming Exercise.

TVSDK: Day 16
Total blockage is achieved. The process of intellectual regeneration begins.

SUCCESS!

The day you finally brick up that last bit of gleaming image will be a milestone in your life. To register this event, on page 81 I have provided a beautiful diploma titled ''The Declaration of TV Independence.'' It is suitable for framing. Remove this page from the book and complete the date and the exact time you flick off the set.

The diploma has blanks for weekly, monthly, and then yearly recertification of your TV independence. In order to fill these out honestly, you must restructure your life without TV. This is explained in the next section.

Congratulate yourself, yes. But keep reading. Rigorous follow-up is essential if you want to stay permanently free of your TV addiction.

C. LIFE AFTER TV

WHAT NOW?

"It really makes me nervous to know that I can't go turn on my set and sit down and watch TV. . . I find myself sitting and staring at the blank TV set."

—A Minnesota housewife
after one week of TV abstinence.

C.1
Life After TV:
Is It Possible?

As you examine the shards of your TV-shattered existence, many bitter ironies will become evident. You are a person who never raised his hand in class. Except for a brief period of adolescent rebellion, you always chose compatible colors in cars, clothing, home furnishings, and friends. In short, you have done your utmost to live a virtually inconspicuous, almost invisible life thus far.

And yet, with the successful completion of the TVSDK treatment, you have thrust yourself into the vanguard of a social revolution quite beyond your wildest Mittyesque fantasy. **This will make you feel very uncomfortable, both physically and emotionally.** Try to take it in stride.

The initial symptoms will be physical, the **TVDTs, or TV Delirium Tremens.** The symptoms — sustained and violent body quavers combined with an unfortunate lack of sphincter control — will not be a pleasant experience. The problem here is that the body is struggling to adapt to a sudden elimination of low-level radiation from the TV set. If you have chosen your postblockage vacation spot prudently (Club Med, for instance, would be all wrong) you will be able to vent these noxious substances into the local environment with a minimum of fuss and worry. Remember, they are all biodegradable.

TV DELIRIUM TREMENS (TVDTs)

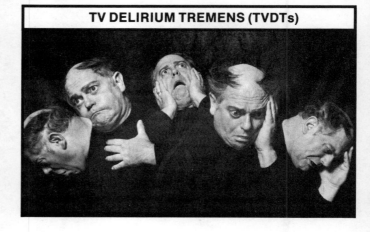

Upon your return to civilization, psychological aberrations will appear. One day you will feel like Donny Osmond on diet pills. Then you will want to be the Flying Nun. These rapid mood swings result from a process called **TV Personality Flushing.**

Try not to resist these impulses. Once you purge yourself of the literally tens of thousands of character surrogates that have been programmed into you by TV, you will be left with the one unique thing you have to offer the world — yourself. If this thought makes you want to throw yourself in front of a city bus, seek reliable counseling right away.

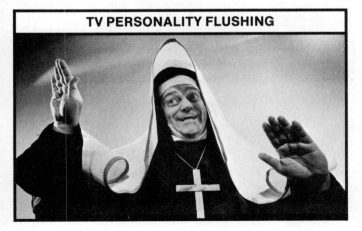

TV PERSONALITY FLUSHING

FIRST SOCIAL CONTACTS

Soon this overt symptomatology will vanish and you'll feel it's safe to appear in public. Be prepared for a big surprise. You will not understand 70 to 95 percent of what is being said. People will be talking about what they saw on TV the previous night. Since you will not yet have learned how to talk naturally — i.e., spontaneous non-TVese — you will have little to do in social groupings besides stand around and look at your shoes.

A great way to fend off this acute sense of social isolation is to prepare a short statement summarizing your recent conversion and to blurt it out whenever you have the chance.

This may seem a bit awkward at first, but it is your only option. You have been cast out into the real world still secretly thinking that GE brings good things to life. But soon you will regard most people's brains as mere jellybean repositories, and this transient period of terror will subside.

C.2
Whither the Box?

You will kill three birds with one stone in this chapter on authorized TV disarmament and disposal procedures. You will neutralize the potential threat of back-sliding in the privacy of your own home. You will express sweet revenge at your former master, the TV set. And you will keep your hands (and what little is left of your mind) busy while you struggle to gain the new social and intellectual skills necessary to make your cure permanent.

Begin by disconnecting the electricity to the set. **Do not attempt to cut through the power cord with scissors, a machete, a hand-held rotary power saw, or your teeth, without first unplugging it.** You don't want to terminate a promising course of treatment in a blinding flash of overpriced voltage.

NEUTERING THE SET

Even after you have pulled the plug, do not think that your TV set will assume a benign role in your everyday appliance life along with the toaster-oven and food processor. For, in order to inflict the necessary violence on the poor unsuspecting electrons that are flung with great speed and accuracy at the phosphor molecules on the back of the picture tube, **very large charges of high voltage electricity are stored up in some of the electronic components and will stay there waiting to zap you even after you pull the plug.** Have your set's innards completely removed by qualified service personnel. Avoid shocks. Play it safe.

WRONG WAY TO NEUTER THE SET

Once you have taken care of this obvious safety hazard, two routes are open to you. You can keep the empty carcass around the house as an object of scorn, or you can dispose of it during a ritual ceremony of your own choosing. In implementing the first option, keep two words in mind, humiliation and practicality.

KEEPING THE SET: HUMILIATION OPTION

Debasing your TV set, while admittedly childish, can help you work out your pent-up rage at having wasted 85 percent of the free time of your life to date.

Drink in the bitter sense of reprisal and the feeling of total control over an object that once held you completely in its sway. Do with it what you will — you're in the driver's seat now.

KEEPING THE SET: RECYCLING OPTION

If you tire of these TV torture sessions but do not yet feel ready to embark on a possibly disorienting round of redecoration decisions, you can remodel your TV for an alternative use. After all, the TV cabinet is in some cases quite a sturdy piece of furniture. Recycling it will assuage your guilt at having wasted so many inflation-shrunken dollars on such a useless investment. Use the following examples for guidance.

A TYPICAL TV TORTURE SESSION

TV DOG HOUSE The console model is especially fitting for use as an outdoor animal habitat. Snug, warm, and up-out-of-the-mud in this lovely twenty-three-inch Sears cabinet, Cap'n surveys his master's yard with an enviable sense of security.

The all-weather, polyethylene flap (shown in its open position) provides an ample supply of light while ensuring that no excess of inclement weather can damage his delicate fur coat or further dilute his waiting bowl of Gravy Train.

TV AQUARIUM There's room to spare in this twenty-one-inch Hartford cabinet adapted for use as a fish condominium.

Frolicking in the frame are a saucy little angel fish, two pugnacious blue gouramis, and the ever popular loach. A sword plant completes the picture. The addition of a few neon tetras would help those who need an outlet for TV nostalgia.

TV NATIVITY SCENE   Looking for a new place to put your crèche this holiday season? Why not use your old TV cabinet for a most dramatic setting? The kids are bound to renew their interest in religion when presented with this charming juxtaposition. These terra-cotta figurines made by the peasant potters of Mexico have been placed on an ordinary terry-cloth towel and set before a plastic wreath.

TV LAUNDRY HAMPER   Get those dirty clothes up off the closet floor and into a spacious TV laundry hamper. You'll never again waste a half-hour looking for that missing sandal when spring rolls around. Just slide your shoes right under the cabinet where they'll stay in plain sight and be handy when you need them. The top surface is a perfect spot for stacking sleeping bags and extra blankets for when your old friends from the sixties drop in unexpectedly.

TV PATIO WALL M. D. McGowan, curator of the Unknown Museum in Mill Valley, California, has combined practicality with an unmistakable sense of visual flair in his forthright construction, above. This TV wall acts as a kind of pedestrian funnel guiding visitors into the front door while neatly masking a service entrance just beyond. *Sunset* magazine will reportedly devote an upcoming issue to the many stunning ways in which old TVs can add to your home's resale value.

GETTING RID OF IT

Eventually you will exhaust your creative ingenuity and find the strength to dispose of your TV set altogether. This will be a landmark in the history of your cultural development. Do not let it slip by without an appropriately elaborate ceremony.

If you wish the event to remain private, select a discreet funeral director and let him take care of everything. If you elect to go ahead with a viewing of the deceased, make sure it's not plugged in.

If you are nostalgic about mass demonstrations, you will want to organize a **Neighborhood TV Destruction Derby.** Simply clear a large area of all trees, shrubs, flowers, plants, and grass. This will be your vast video wasteland. Then schedule a time convenient for all. Stack all the TV sets in a pile in the center. Then, after a short invocation by a local minister, priest, or rabbi, proceed to destroy the sets in a manner most befitting your group sense of rage. You will be left with a lovely anti-TV theme park to commemorate the occasion.

MEDIA BURN: A PIONEERING WORK OF TV SELF-DEFENSE

"The Phantom Dream Car crashes through a wall of burning TV sets at the Cow Palace in San Francisco, July 4, 1975: *Media Burn* was a performance created and produced by Ant Farm (Lord, Michels, Schreier) and staged before video cameras and a live audience. The resulting videotape has been exhibited widely in an art context. It has never, however, been broadcast on television."—Chip Lord

Photo: Diane Hall

C.3
Learning New Skills

Sooner or later every reformed TV addict must face up to the ultimate question: What am I going to do with all my free time? This can be devastating, especially when you realize that the lack of a reasonable answer to this question is probably at the root of your TV addiction in the first place. You will look into your life and find the hours previously taken up with TV staring back at you like some bottomless chasm. You might even feel like jumping.

Take solace in the fact that this has been a problem for every species with an overdeveloped cerebral hemisphere. It is the eternal dilemma of boredom: What do you do when the chores necessary for survival are out of the way and your instinctual appetites are sated but you're still not tired?

Realizing that available leisure time was bound to increase with the rise of civilization, many hardy entrepreneurs have invented countless diversions for the mind and body during one's time off: grain alcohol, religion, games of chance, and great books. From tiddlywinks to tennis, the opportunities are enormous.

The problem is that you have experienced most of these things only vicariously — on television. So you are bound to be a little nervous about actually doing them, live and in person.

Even more disturbing will be your tendency to try to emulate role models from the tube. You will be genuinely upset that you can't serve like Björn Borg or say silly things charmingly while perched upside-down in your Calvins like Brooke Shields.

The most prudent bet is to begin practicing your new TV-replacement skills in the privacy of your own home, away from the baleful glare of public sanction.

A good way to start is by **Reading,** something at which you have already demonstrated moderate competence by getting this far in my book. Try to ignore your initial allergic response to reading. The symptoms range from the simple inability to focus on written words to a total incomprehension of tricky concepts like consecutive page numbers.

The problem is that you will be encountering things like complex sentences and paragraphs for the first time since your school days. Reading "Spray 'n Wash gets out what America gets into" does not prepare you for such advanced syntactic difficulties.

So start out slowly, with something like your local tabloid newspaper. When you find a word you do not understand, stop and look it up in the dictionary. Test your comprehension skills by summarizing any articles you do manage to finish. Remember, you now have plenty of time, so speed is not important.

Soon you will find yourself climbing back up the literacy ladder and tackling more strenuous works like *Newsweek* and *Family Circle.* Now would be a good time to schedule a visit to your local Public Library.

INITIAL PROBLEMS WITH READING

Libraries have a kind of *TV Guide* for books called the card catalogue. Every book has a number listed on a file card along with the title, author, and subject matter. When you locate a book listing that interests you, you don't have to wait until a certain time for the book to come on, like on TV. You just go into the "stacks," the rows of bookcases, and follow the number system until you find the one you want.

This random access to books is a wonderful thing. You can go to any book in the library whenever a whim beckons. When you get there you can poke through it and see if it suits your taste. Then stay with it or strike out for something else. You do it at your own pace and in your own direction. This is called **Learning.**

Many think of TV as a prime tool of learning. But think about the differences between TV and reading. TV offers short subjects on a limited range of topics. They are preprogrammed to appear on a schedule that you cannot alter. And when they finally do come on, you have to consume them from one end to the other, in a fixed sequence determined by the show's producer. You can't taste a TV show at your own rate, bypassing parts that don't appeal and concentrating on what interests you. You're stuck with it for the duration, usually hoping that it'll get better in the end.

This is not a process designed to make us into a nation of independent thinkers. Does somebody want it that way? Does anybody know what this process is doing to us? These are good questions. I'm sure you'll have to go to the library for the answers.

> 66 No sane parent would present a child with a fire engine, snatch it away in thirty seconds, replace it with a set of blocks, snatch that away thirty seconds later, replace the blocks with clay, and then replace the clay with a toy car. Yet in effect, a young child receives that kind of experience when he or she watches American television. 55
>
> Drs. Dorothy and Jerome Singer (co-directors of the Yale Family Television Research and Consultation Center in New Haven), quoted by Kate Moody in "The Research on TV: A Disturbing Picture," *New York Times,* April 20, 1980.

AT LEAST GIVE ME A MINUTE WITH THE BLOCKS

Another good place to find interesting books is the bookstore. They look very much like libraries but when you find a book you like you have to pay for it before taking it home. If you do this enough, you will develop your own mini-library. This can be an excellent place in which to drink rum and spend your old age.

Sooner or later your new fountain of knowledge will begin to overflow and you will want to learn how to **Talk** intelligently. Try to avoid talking to people who are still under the influence, however. You will find these people, like TV itself, full of little bits of useless information that they do not understand. Carl Sagan clones (Type PBS) are among the worst offenders. They will expect you to respond with the same misty-eyed, in-awe-of-the-infinite-universe look that they so shamelessly exhibit. You can easily bring these people back to Earth with a quick review of, say, the *Consumer Reports* analysis of compact station wagons.

Using just these two skills, reading and talking, you will begin to **Make New Friends,** a strange and wonderful circumstance of life that many people give up for good at about age twenty-two. You will attend adult-education classes. You will be invited to parties. Some people will consider you to be an oddity because you can tell them the size of the federal budget but don't know the size of Nancy Reagan's shoes. Be patient. Try to ease into a new relationship by offering a gift copy of the TVSDK.

Even if you think you have not the least bit of talent, **Music** is still a wonderful activity. Listening to music is OK, but like TV, it demands little participation. So try to become active in music. This is something that peo-

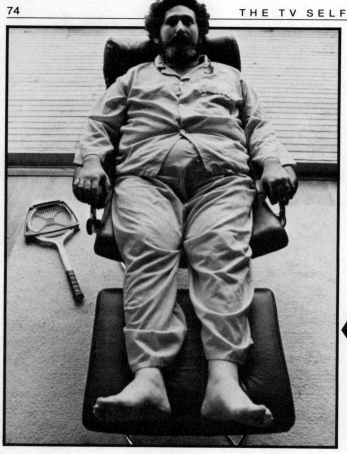

ple used to do more in the olden days. It helped dispel that nagging fear that the sky was about to collapse. It could do the same for you. And besides, you can dance to it too.

While on the subject of nagging fears, let's not forget about **Religion.** TV has supplanted much religious participation. This is in part because you can now have that lame arm worked over by a TV faith healer at the screen of your set. But if God is a turn-on for you, why not get out and go to church? You can be sure that you will be greeted warmly, at least at first, because newcomers are scarce these days in many churches.

Another childhood skill you'll want to renew is participatory **Sports.** Kids are usually natural athletes until they're old enough to not make the team. But take away the competitive pressures and you'll find yourself enjoying games you'd given up years ago.

Be sure to consult with your doctor before initiating any strenuous exercise. Remember, your body has assumed the shape of a Barcalounger. You may not be able to do the things you once did without some careful planning and probably a scaling down of personal standards. Try to play for the fun of it. When this stops happening, either give it up or get really serious and try to make some money at it.

As the blood flow increases to parts of the body you forgot existed, you will want to start having **Sex** again. Like religion, sex is something in which most people lost interest during their TV-induced-stupor days. But between consenting adults, it is a relaxing and low-cost way to wile away the prime-time hours.

Try to avoid comparisons with TV stars. Your partner may not be as beautiful as Morgan Fairchild or as rich as Larry Hagman. But your partner is the one in bed with you. Make the most of what you've got.

Politics is another interesting way to spend your time. People once felt that TV would lead to some form of perfect democracy. Everyone would be exposed to the entire political process and begin to take a more active role in its workings. This was before Richard Nixon lost an election because of bad makeup and a sincere old actor from California got the role of a lifetime: commander in chief, for real.

Voting percentages have been declining since the TV generation reached the age of majority in the mid-sixties. So your participation here will be as unexpected and welcome as it was in church.

Go to your local town meetings. Then you can find out firsthand if the country really is being run by idiots, as some have suggested.

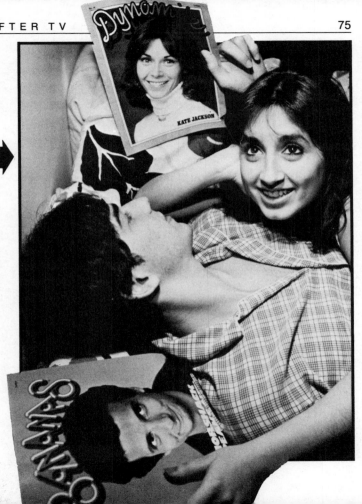

C.4
Kids

There is little doubt that children are the most pathetic victims of TV addiction. Little personalities in a tremendous state of flux have an instinctive tendency to soak up whatever is presented — without much critical scrutiny. The results of this perfectly natural process depend largely on what we older people choose to expose them to.

Our primitive ancestors learned their survival skills from direct observation of the world around them. To run like the hare, to slither like the snake, to be as still as a deer worried about getting an arrow in the neck — these useful traits were learned by imitation of the local scene. Now kids learn how to ride their trail bikes like California Highway Patrolmen in hot pursuit, talk like Bugs Bunny, and stretch body tendons like Mean Joe Greene. Parents, understandably, are getting worried.

Kids have a perversely effective way of getting what they think they want. If you find it difficult to submit your child to the TVSDK treatment, try the following experiment. Dubbed **The Silverman Box,** I developed it in response to the news that RCA is working on a TV set that dispenses Ring Dings and Sugar Snaps, on demand.

Find a child who is just old enough to play by himself — a two-year-old is ideal. Place him in a room with all of his favorite toys and a TV set that you can remote control. Station yourself in an adjoining room.

Now observe. Unless he is hungry, tired, or spoiled beyond belief, the kid will commence having a great time doing what outwardly appears to be the dumbest things — sucking on the wheels of his stroller, tasting a three-week-old piece of pizza that is lodged between the bars of his xylophone, constructing an elaborate pillow house, and so on.

This is called learning by doing. The kid is experimenting with his world by exploring the materials at hand. He's exercising his brain and his body — even now practicing for the day he might have to decide between law school and an MBA. Wince as you may, this activity is good for the child. Dr. Spock will back me up on this.

Now turn on the set and watch what happens. As if stunned by a cattle prod, the child will cease all body movement and flop down on the nearest horizontal surface. Like a leaf that heeds the call of phototropism, he will orient his face toward the screen.

He will remain motionless in this position until something really boring like a viewer editorial comes on. Then he will sigh deeply, make a torpid survey of the room, and turn back to the TV.

This child has signed off for the duration. His mind is on vacation. His body is turning into jelly. He has very little chance of becoming the kind of person who makes it through the Sunday paper in less than three days.

If you have an iron will, proceed with the final stage of the experiment. Open the door to the room and scream the child's name as loud as you can. Now act like you are being eaten by a pack of wolves. He will not respond.

Next, place three partially melted gallons of his favorite ice cream in his lap, and coat the ice cream and his forearms with pancake syrup and chocolate sauce. Introduce live animals into the room: a dog, white mice, a bird with a broken wing in a shoebox — use whatever is handy. Finally send in the child's mother dressed as Iggy the Clown and have her do cartwheels, some juggling, and a fast-paced puppet show.

The child will move only to clear his path of vision to the screen. When you turn it off he will scream bloody murder until you force-feed him a bottle of grape juice heavily laced with Valium.

TYPICAL CHILD ADDICT

This should be convincing. But no matter what rationale brings them to include their children in the TVSDK process, parents must expect to have hell to pay during the following period. Imagine how David Stockman would feel if we suddenly told him to stop working on the federal budget.

> 66 Recently Dr. Benjamin Spock brought his stepdaughter and granddaughter to New York for a tour of the Bronx Zoo and the Museum of Modern Art. But the man who has the prescription for everything from diaper rash to bed-wetting could not dislodge the kids from their hotel room. 'I couldn't get them away from the goddamn TV set,' recalls Spock. 'It made me sick.' 99
>
> Harry F. Waters, "What TV Does to Kids," *Newsweek*, February 21, 1977.

SPOCK SOCKED BY FAMILY ADDICTION

TV is a kind of Rosetta stone of present-day childhood culture. Its denial will seriously impair a child's ability to decipher most current forms of socially acceptable small people's behavior. Be prepared to use military tactics in the battle for your child's mind.

When in doubt, think about the overwhelming benefits that will accrue: a strong, healthy body, the desire and ability to think about things other than rock stars, dramatically lower dentist bills, and a complete erasure of the phrase "You deserve a break today" from your child's memory bank.

Many parents become depressed when their children fall into a clinical state of **Catatonia** before they can sign their names on the Declaration of TV Independence. They know that intravenous-feeding techniques are not the kind of thing one learns in just one afternoon.

Try to be understanding. Your child is not moving, because he can't think of what to do. This is because he has rarely, if ever, had to. You have pulled the plug on his entire identity structure. Do not expect him to light up again until you teach him to think for himself. Remember your own struggles with this problem. With you it was redevelopment. With him it's like Genesis, chapter 1, verse 1.

Parents of young children will have to arrange for a **Big Bird Ritual Burial Ceremony.** This purgative event is the only known method for extricating small minds from a pathological identification with *Sesame Street.*

When *Sesame Street* hit the screens of public-television in 1969, critics promptly hailed it as a giant step in the quest to harness TV as a universal educational medium. But few people stopped to think what would happen to a nursery-school teacher who insisted on dressing up like funny animals and changed the subject every two minutes.

As the show's novelty began to wear thin during the seventies, many parents realized that while *Sesame Street* was certainly a revolutionary development in baby-sitting, its educational value might not be all that had been claimed. Others wondered how a noncommercial TV show could so effectively drain previously ample toy budgets.

Even though your child has stopped watching TV, you must realize that a fifth column of Sesame symbols has already jumped out of the TV set into his room. They are waiting there to tempt him into massive regression. Your job is to undertake a meticulous search-and-destroy mission to obliterate every last vestige of his former Muppet-infested lifestyle.

The Last Word

For some of you, the purchase of this book has given you something otherwise unavailable anywhere or at any price — more time in your life. You have cured your TV addiction, endured the difficult transition phase, and now pursue those things that truly interest you without first checking *TV Guide.* Congratulations. You deserve all the credit.

For others, the tale has not been so happy. You have reached the mountaintop and tasted TV freedom only to have it snatched out of your hands by impulses that seem beyond your self-control. Even now as you plod through the last pages of this book at a speed of twenty words per hour, you are watching an episode of *Gilligan's Island* that you have seen at least five times.

In either case, I have one final request: Write to me about your personal struggle with TV addiction. Please.

For those who have been successful, this process will be a final validation of your considerable achievement. In addition, "going public" with your story will make you think twice about slipping back into your previous life of abject videocy. For those less fortunate, I hope only that you will discover an untapped inner resolve during the many hours it takes you to complete this exercise.

For me, your true-life stories will be the basis for further research into the world's most widespread yet least understood epidemic of mental debility. If I receive enough responses, I will try to have representative excerpts published in a companion volume titled something like: *Son of TVSDK: The People Talk Back.* If, on the other hand, I receive less than, say, ten letters, my wife will have a much easier time convincing me to go into another line of work.

So if you care about a TV-free future, write to me:

Mike Haller
c/o Houghton Mifflin Company
2 Park Street
Boston, Massachusetts 02108

Thanks for listening.

Declaration of TV Independence

for

_____
(Print name here)

Whereas the undersigned has successfully completed the TVSDK treatment program, achieving total screen blockage in _____ days; and

Whereas the undersigned has turned off his TV set at the time and date specified below for what he/she solemnly promises to be the last time;

It is hereby declared that the undersigned has entered into a presumably perpetual state of TV independence.

TV Turn Off:_____, 19___; _____AM/PM   _____
                       (date)   (time—circle one)   (Sign name or make mark here)

Recertification Box   I hereby certify that I have been completely TV-free for:

1 Week	____(Initials)	___(Date)____	6 Months	___(Initials)	__(Date)____
2 Weeks ____	____	____	1 Year ____	____	____
1 Month ____	____	____	2 Years ____	____	____
2 Months____	____	____	3 Years ____	____	____

THE TV SELF-DEFENSE KIT

TVSDKard and Portaquote Guide

There are thirty TVSDKards and nine inspirational Portaquotes about TV in the following pages. Assuming the publisher has done a half-decent job of binding, you will have to remove these pages from the book with your X-Acto Knife or single-edge razor. Again, remember to **be careful.** Personal injury at this critical stage would be a setback.

Place the book on your TVSDK Work Station. Bend it back to expose the inside edge of the facing page (page 83). Now cut through this page as close to the binding as possible. Repeat this process on each of the remaining odd-numbered pages (pages 85 and 87, etc.). When you finish, you will have removed the six pages of TVSDKard blanks and the final page of Portaquotes.

First, cut out the Portaquotes and mount them conspicuously in your home, place of work, school, or other location. Remember, the more people become interested in the TVSDK treatment, the less lonely you'll feel when you finally stop watching.

Next, assemble the remains of the six pages that contain the TVSDKards, five to a page. Cut these out with your scissors, trimming off the white borders. You have produced a neat little stack of thirty TVSDKards.

When you are ready to begin the Total Blockage Sequence (TBS, page 57) you must prepare the Kards for mounting. Cut off a piece of double-stick adhesive tape that is slightly longer than the long dimension of the Kard. Stick this onto the back of the Kard in the middle and fold the protruding tabs around the front. This will ensure that the tape stays put on the Kards if you need to remove some during a backsliding episode.

A note on the TVSDKard design:

I originally wanted the cards to be made of thin black opaque plastic, which will actually stick to the magnetic field on the surface of the TV screen without using tape. After a long and rarely cordial discussion with the publisher's representatives I was convinced that if I wanted the plastic Kards I could go and publish the book myself. I capitulated to their position.

If enough people request it, I will try to arrange to have TVSD Kustom Kard Kits fabricated by a reputable manufacturer. Send your requests to the address listed on page 80.

TVSDK Portaquote "Technically, TV is beyond my expectation. But the programs! I would never let my children even come close to this thing. It's awful what they're doing." —Vladimir K. Zworykin, inventor of the TV tube in 1923

From "TV Turns Off Its Father," <u>New York Times</u>, July 31, 1981, p. B16.

TVSDK Portaquote "About a year ago I tried to make my life like a television show. When I get mad at my sister I try to make it feel like a soap opera. A few minutes later I'll get sad and hug her and say I'm sorry, real dramatic, like on TV." —Sandy, twelve, student

...om "Television and Our Private ...ves," by Jeanne Betancourt, ...annels, December 1981– ...nuary 1982, p. 51.

TVSDK Portaquote "It wasn't like on TV. When I stabbed him the knife would only go in a little way. He wouldn't die." —Convicted teen-age murderer explaining why he stabbed his eleven-year-old victim twenty-two times

m "Naive Murder Plan
d to TV Violence," by Barry
gel, Los Angeles Times,
uary 2, 1980, p 28.

TVSDK Portaquote "[The challenge today is to turn the home] from an area of social gatherings for friends into a center of electronic communications and entertainment." —Jack Sauter, vice-president and general manager of RCA Consumer Electronics

m "Gritty Optimism for a
k Biz in Search of a Market,"
teve Knoll, <u>Variety</u>, October
1980, p. 53.

TVSDK Portaquote "Television has affected our sex life. We stay up watching television, then just go to sleep because we're tired. If we had gone to bed earlier we probably would have made love." —Mary, research physiologist

"Television and Our Private [Lives]" by Jeanne Betancourt, [Chan]nels, December 1981– [Janu]ary 1982, p. 50.

TVSDK

TVSDK

TVSDK

TVSDK Portaquote "My father thinks it's dumb to give up TV. He says TV's his best friend. I said, 'Maybe it isn't.' But he wasn't listening." —A nine-year-old New Jersey girl who quit watching TV for one week as part of a school project

TVSDK

TVSDK

om "Vidiots Anonymous," Steve McNamara and Liz lhelm, <u>Pacific Sun</u>, January -21, 1982, p. 6.

TVSDK Portaquote "Many more heavy TV viewers than light TV viewers—living in the same neighborhoods, being the same age, the same sex, having the same income, the same occupation—will say: 'Yes, I've bought a new lock,' or 'Yes, I've bought a new watchdog,' or 'Yes, I bought a new gun for protection.'

"They live in a meaner and more dangerous world than their next-door neighbors who watch less television. So they get a sense of insecurity, which implies dependence on the authorities.

"Probably the most disturbing part of it is the implication that these insecure people—those whose notions about the world and the dangers in the world have been cultivated by the frequency of violence on television—will accept repression, even welcome repression, if it comes in the name of security." —Dr. George Gerbner, dean, Annenberg School of Communications, University of Pennsylvania

Gerbner quoted from "The Television Explosion," <u>Nova</u>, February 14, 1982 (show no. 906).

TVSDK Portaquote "Television is called a medium because nothing it serves up is ever well done." —Jack Benny

Benny quoted from "What TV Does to Kids," by Harry F. Waters, <u>Newsweek</u>, February 21, 1977, p. 69.

TVSDK Portaquote "The trouble with the creative people is that they don't know the public. The people out there don't want to think. [They want more] broads, boobs and busts." —James T. Aubrey, Jr., president of CBS-TV from December 1959 to February 1965

Aubrey quoted from <u>The Powers that Be</u>, by David Halberstam (New York: Dell, 1980), p. 358. (Originally published by Alfred A. Knopf in 1979.)

TVSDK Portaquote "This show is so light that it would take a week to get to the ground if you dropped it from the ceiling." —Kate Jackson commenting on the quality of <u>Charlie's Angels</u> scripts

Jackson quoted from "Farewell to a Phenomenon," by Otto Friedrich, <u>Time</u>, June 8, 1981, p. 73.